A Miracle of Life

Stories of a Warrior and Triumphant Boy

Inés López de Lara Ahued

A Miracle of Life

ISBN: 979-8-9941642-0-4

Published by Light of Life Books

Printed in the United States of America

I was born in the beautiful state of Michoacan, Mexico and grew up in the majestic city of Zacatecas. I studied Early Childhood Education and specialized as an

 English Teacher at La Salle University in Cancun. Years later, I graduated from the University of South Florida with a concentration in Spanish as a Foreign Language.

I am a very proud mother of three precious children and have three adorable grandchildren. My passion is music. I play piano and guitar, and I enjoy writing songs. My mission in life is to be happy and bring joy to others, based on my faith in God. I have been blessed with angels who have brightened my path in the journey of my life, which inspired me to write my first book, "A Miracle of Life."

First, I want to thank God for giving me life and with it great blessings. For blessing me with a wonderful family whom I love with all my heart and who are invaluable human beings.

For giving me three children, who are the constant source of my happiness. For their love which they have bestowed upon me since they were little. For the joy of seeing them grow and transform into extraordinary and successful individuals.

For giving me an exemplary mother, who taught me to believe in Him above all else, and thanks to that unwavering faith, I am here to tell you about the incredible magical events that made my son's life and existence possible in this book that I have titled "A Miracle of Life."

I also want to express my heartfelt gratitude to my daughter, Jaclyn Elizabeth, whose loving guidance and thoughtful support accompanied me throughout the creation of this book. Her presence was a blessing on this journey.

Index

Chapter 1

Seeds of Faith:
My Identity, My Family, and My Mother's Legacy

Let me begin by telling you a little about my life: I come from a beautiful family, five sisters, two brothers, and an exemplary mother. My mom always taught us that in life, God comes first, and after Him, family is the most important thing.

When we were children, our family was very close-knit. Always ready to support each other in any circumstance that arose. We were like a team of players, each with our position on the field of life.

Bound by indestructible bonds, we overflowed with vitality, joy, and fun in every game we played together. All of this, thanks to the tireless efforts of our beautiful mom, who with unwavering love, watched over our well-being and happiness, being our star coach in this game called life.

My mom, recognizing education's vital role, instilled in us a commitment to academic excellence. She coupled this with strong values and a sense of responsibility, guiding each of us to complete our studies and achieve our goals. But beyond all that, she instilled in us an unwavering faith in God for which I will be eternally grateful, as this teaching shaped my life and the extraordinary and indescribable miracles of my son's life that I will share later in this book.

Later, as is the law of life, each of us, brothers and sisters, embarked on our own path. Destiny led us to places we had never imagined, much less thought we would ever live there.

Sadly, life took us down different paths, physically separating us, but always maintaining the bonds of love and shared memories. And I say "sadly" because family always leaves a void when they are not nearby, and that feeling of longing is difficult to mitigate. But the key is to carry each other in our hearts, and that's how we soften that feeling of sadness.

Even so, to this day, whenever we have the opportunity to visit or gather, it's a joyous occasion and the excitement is overwhelming. It's as if time stands still and we become that united team full of life and joy that we once were. But now with more players. Because we are no longer just seven, the family has grown and multiplied. This is another great testament to the existence of God, as each new life, each new family member, is unique and incomparable in the essence of their being.

With those solid foundations created in our lives, I made the decision to start my own family. God blessed me with the joy of being a mother to three beautiful children whom I adore. Three beautiful grandchildren who have filled my life with abundant joy, and two sons-in-law whom I admire, love, and respect.

Life itself is *The Wonder of Creation*, and we, without a doubt, are *God's Masterpiece*.

And that's how I share with you a little of our history, full of love, growth, and blessings that remind us of the divine greatness in every step of life's journey united in one heart.

Chapter 2

A New Life, A New Dawn:
Blessings Multiply

It was April 1997, and we were living in Playa del Carmen, Mexico. I was happily married to Denny, an American guy of Polish descent from Baltimore. He was a very cheerful, fun-loving man with a big heart. We had two beautiful daughters, Jessica Lizeth who was seven and Jaclyn Elizabeth who was two. They were both lovely girls with unique personalities, full of joy and fun. Since we lived by the beach, they loved playing in the sand and going for a swim. I was the director of a school, and Denny worked in a scuba shop. It was a spectacular and very touristy place. A true paradise!

One day, my sister Lucía wanted to visit us and spend her vacation with us. So the day came, and Jessica

Lizeth and Jaclyn Elizabeth were very excited to go with me to pick her up at the airport. She would stay with us for a week, so every day we would enjoy the beautiful and sunny beaches together. Lucía loved watching the sunrise on the beach. So one of those days, we decided to join her and enjoy the magnificent sight together.

With great enthusiasm, we got up very early and headed to the beach to witness the sunrise. Despite being sleepy, Jessica and Jaclyn were very happy and full of energy. At that age, children are full of life, they love to have fun and experience new things. For them, getting up at five in the morning to go to the beach was quite an adventure.

We hurried along the way, knowing that the sunrise was approaching quickly. It was five-thirty in the morning, and we didn't want to miss a single second of the spectacle that nature had prepared for us. The sun would start to rise at five-fifty, and we were eager to witness that magical moment. Since Lucía was pregnant, sometimes she couldn't walk as fast, and we would burst into laughter because she would say, "Run! Run, the sun is about to come out!" And we would run while she lagged behind. So we had to stop and wait for her. It was very funny. We were all running and laughing. It was a fantastically fun morning.

We arrived at the beach just as the sun began to rise with immense splendor. A true wonder. Life is beautiful, especially when you feel that gratitude to God for seeing the light of each morning and so much beauty that the Universe offers us day by day. We felt very happy to have arrived on time. So we sat down for a while in the sand to bask in nature's breathtaking display.

Meanwhile, Jessica and Jaclyn happily started playing at the edge of the sea. While they played, Lucía and I talked about so many beautiful things in life. About the beauty of being a mother and at the same time, the great responsibility that this implied. The miracle of the life of a new being that comes into the world, defenseless, depending one hundred percent on its mother to survive. How wonderful! How wonderful life is! Undoubtedly, a gift from God, the life of a new being. Children are the ultimate creation, they are *God's masterpiece*. We were both very happy and grateful to God for being chosen to be mothers.

Days went by, and Lucía had to return to Zacatecas. The air at the airport was charged with emotions as we said our goodbyes. Her visit was amazing, as we shared wonderful and unforgettable moments.

A few weeks after Lucía had left, I suspected I might be pregnant with my third child. So, I decided to take a test. Indeed, another baby was on the way! The test came back positive. I couldn't believe it. I was so delighted that tears of excitement filled my eyes, tears of happiness, tears announcing the arrival of a new being. I was sure I would love this new baby with the same intensity as my two beautiful girls, with all my heart. I never would have imagined that while Lucía and I shared our excitement about my new niece, and the joy of motherhood, I was already pregnant with my third child.

Without wasting a second, I shared the news with Denny, who couldn't contain his excitement upon hearing it. "Another child? You must be joking! Are you serious?" "Yes!" I replied excitedly. "Really! It's true!" "I hope it's a boy!" He said with much emotion. He was overflowing with happiness. What a thrilling and surprising moment for us both. So, with my heart pounding with excitement, I picked up the phone and called Lucía. "You won't believe what I'm going to tell you!" "What?" she responded with curiosity. Without further ado, I told her the big news: "I'm pregnant too!" "No way!" she exclaimed, "I don't believe you!" Amidst the uncertainty of whether I was joking or not, I could hear and feel her choking back tears of joy and excitement.

Meanwhile, I found myself equally overwhelmed, crying my own tears of happiness as I shared this wonderful news. "When is the due date?" she asked me. "In January, God willing. I'm two months along," I replied. The excitement was such that neither of us could believe it. We would have wanted to be together to celebrate and hug each other, but we were so far apart. However, despite the distance that separated us, the connection between us was tangible through the phone line. We both longed to be together again. The excitement emanating from her voice resonated in my heart, filling me with joy and gratitude for this beautiful gift of life. Two sisters, pregnant at the same time!

As soon as I finished talking to her, I also called my mom and I couldn't contain my excitement. She was overjoyed, although at the same time a little sad not to be able to be with me at that moment to embrace me and celebrate the good news. I will always remember her sweet words when she said to me, "With all my heart, I wish I could be there with you. But God will provide, I will see you soon. In the meantime, I promise you that I will buy yarn to start knitting a little blanket for the baby today."

My mom had always liked to knit. She knitted beautiful sweaters, blankets, and scarves. She could make anything. And when it came to her grandchildren, her creations were the most beautiful. So, she got to work. I was very happy to hear her words, besides I knew that knitting the little sweaters and blankets kept her busy and excited. Life isn't easy when families are separated, but fate separated us, and we had to learn to live far from each other but always *united in one heart*. That was my mantra.

My mom happily took it upon herself to share the news with my other siblings, which also brought them immense joy, knowing of the arrival of a new being to the family. And now, I had to tell my girls the news. I could already imagine how happy they would be, as I picked them up from school. So, I went to get them, and when we arrived home, I said, "Guess what? I have super exciting news for you!" "What is it, Mom?" Jessica Lizeth asked. "You're going to have a new sister or a new brother!" They both ran and embraced me so happily and excitedly. They started jumping for joy. "I want it to be a little brother," said Jessica Lizeth. "Me too, and when he's born, I want him to be named Winnie the Pooh," chimed Jaclyn Elizabeth.

Everyone started laughing. It was very funny. Jaclyn was quite amusing. Then Jessica said, "I want him to be named Denny Michael." And Jaclyn insisted, "No, Mommy, I want him to be named Winnie the Pooh." Jessica, Denny, and I couldn't stop laughing. "Well," I said, "let's see. We'll decide once he's born because we still don't know if it's going to be a boy or a girl." "Well, I already know it's going to be a boy," said Jessica. Jaclyn quickly affirmed, "Me too." Those were precious moments that stayed with us forever.

So the days went by, and every day I took all the care that a pregnancy requires. If I ever had a headache or didn't feel very well, I never took any kind of medicine or anything that could harm the baby. I had done the same with my other pregnancies, and thankfully, had not had any problems with either of the two girls. Both of my pregnancies had been completely normal, and I never faced any complications. So I was sure that everything would be fine with the third one.

I started going to routine medical check-ups, and later on, I had an ultrasound. The doctor told me that everything looked good, so there was nothing to worry about. It was that day that we found out the baby was a boy. Jessica and Jaclyn were absolutely thrilled with the news. We were all overjoyed. I continued with the routine care, eating healthy, exercising, and taking prenatal vitamins. We were all so excited that we couldn't wait for the day of the baby's arrival into the world. However, we had to wait and enjoy the anticipation.

Chapter 3

A Providential Encounter

Several months went by, and the eagerly awaited day was approaching. So, since we were living in Playa del Carmen, I remembered the decision I had previously made that if I ever had another baby, he would be born in the United States for the ease of arranging the birth certificate and passport. Given my two previous experiences, I didn't think twice about it.

Although traveling to the United States involved a significant expense, as we would need to buy several plane tickets, I was certain that I would find a way to manage it. Although I shouldn't worry, as my mom always said, "God will provide." So Denny and I talked about it, and he agreed. However, he wouldn't be able to accompany us at the moment, as it was peak season and his work hadn't authorized him to take leave until the second week of January. So we decided to spend Christmas together and leave the next day. So I started making preparations for the trip.

On December 22nd, it was a Monday, the girls and I went to the travel agency to make the reservation. When we entered, there was a lady sitting at her desk, and I said, "Good afternoon, I need to make a reservation, please." The lady looked astonished and asked me, "Are you traveling?" "Yes," I replied, "I need three tickets to Baltimore, Maryland, please. One adult and two children." "But you're pregnant, and you're not allowed to travel after seven months of pregnancy," she replied. "Oh, that's no problem then," I told her. "My baby is due in March." "Oh, okay," the lady said. "Then there's no problem." I had to tell a little white lie, in reality, there were only three weeks left, and that wasn't going to stop me from traveling. So she gave me the prices, and I told her to make the reservation for Friday, December 26th. It was nine hundred dollars. The tickets cost three hundred each, and we only had six hundred.

So I asked the lady if she could make the reservation for me, and I would come back later to pay. Then she said, "With pleasure, but you only have two days because we'll close on the 24th at noon for Christmas." At that moment, I still didn't know how I was going to do it, but with much confidence, I said, "Perfect, thank you very much. I'll come on Wednesday before noon to pay." I was aware that between Denny and me, we only had six hundred dollars to our name, but I was sure that God would give me the light and help me find a way to make up the difference.

These days, a well-managed credit card could have solved this problem, but back then, neither of us had one. So I still had to figure out how to solve and get the money for the other ticket.

The only way was to borrow it. Although borrowing money was something I had never done in my life. Because something very important that my mom taught us and that I always appreciate was to work to solve economic problems and be independent. However, at that moment, it wasn't the case. I needed help from someone. But from whom? God would provide the solution.

I didn't want to turn to my mom or my siblings because I knew deep down it wasn't something urgent. It was just a whim on my part to want to go to the United States to facilitate the birth certificate and passport procedures. Although I'm sure if I had told them, they would have found a way to help me one way or another. But it was going to be Christmas, and I knew everyone had their own expenses, let alone adding another three hundred dollars, which was a lot at that time. So I had to think of another solution because I was determined for the baby to be born in the United States and didn't want to give up on the idea.

That afternoon, when Denny came home from work, I told him about it, and as we both thought about how we could solve it, suddenly it came to my mind, Roni!

"I know who can help us! Roni!"

Roni was an American friend who attended AA meetings with Denny. Every time she saw us, she kindly said to me, "If you ever need anything, don't hesitate to ask me." Then Denny said, Oh no, the AA meetings are over, and we don't go back until January. I don't know where she lives. It's very likely that she's already gone back to the States." "Oh well, there's not much we can do about that," I said sadly, because Roni was the only person at that moment whom I would trust to ask for such a favor, and I was sure she would have helped us. But there was no way to know where to find her.

"Well," I thought again, "God will give us the solution." I couldn't help feeling sad because I didn't know what to do. However, the last thing I could lose was my faith, and I wouldn't allow that. At that time, cell phones had just begun to emerge, and they were very expensive. There wasn't the ease of communication that exists today. No idea how to contact her.

So I went to sleep, asking God with all my faith to enlighten me and give me the answer. I knew he would help me find the solution to know how to get the money we were missing because I only had one day left to pay for the tickets, and that would determine where the baby would be born, whether in the United States or Mexico. And that was definitely in God's hands.

In the journey of life, we often find ourselves holding onto hopes and dreams that appear to be beyond our reach, causing moments of despair. We yearn for everything to fall into place seamlessly, for divine intervention to provide solutions exactly as we envision them and precisely when we deem fit. However, reality often diverges from these idealized scenarios. It's during these times that placing our trust in a higher power becomes paramount. Understanding that the unfolding of events is ultimately guided by a divine plan offers solace amidst life's uncertainties. Each twist and turn, every outcome, carries the imprint of a greater purpose, reminding us that God holds the ultimate authority.

Thus, surrendering to this belief brings peace, knowing that whatever transpires is orchestrated by a force far greater than our own desires and expectations.

As the days unfolded, we found ourselves awaiting answers, knowing that time held the key to our uncertainties. If destiny had decreed that our child would come into the world in the United States, we held firm in the belief that divine guidance would illuminate our path and provide the necessary means. Thus, there existed no room for worry or doubt; our faith remained steadfast.

The next day, Tuesday, December 23rd, arrived with a hint of anticipation in the air. Denny rose early and headed off to work. Jessica and Jaclyn were bubbling with excitement about the birthday party they'd been invited to, though their enthusiasm was tinged with a touch of worry about the weather. Observing their expressive little faces, I reflected, *"In life, you have to overcome all the obstacles that come your way."* Despite the sky being overcast and the looming threat of rain, I was determined not to let it dampen their spirits. Their eyes shone with such excitement that a few clouds weren't going to stand in our way.

Clad in our finest attire, armed with umbrellas as a precaution, we embarked on our mission to buy the perfect gift for the occasion, as we would then take a taxi to Playacar where the party was being held.

We set out well ahead of schedule, mindful that the party was scheduled for two o'clock. Thus, by a quarter to two, we found ourselves stationed outside the store with the gift waiting at the taxi stand. Then, it started drizzling and suddenly, a heavy storm began. One could see the girls were worried, as they had been looking forward to their friend's party for several days. There wasn't a single taxi in sight. Some passed by, but all were full. Thirty minutes passed, and the rain continued, the girls' faces looked a bit sad. I encouraged them, saying, "Don't worry, I'm sure a taxi will come soon." But nothing, taxis passed by but were all occupied. Time kept ticking away and we were still standing there waiting for a taxi.

At two-thirty, the rain persisted relentlessly, with no taxi in sight. Another fifteen minutes trickled by, inching closer to three o'clock. With a heavy heart, I addressed the girls, expressing my regret, "I'm sorry, girls, we'll wait just five more minutes. If a taxi doesn't arrive, we may have to concede that we won't make it to the party, considering it started at two." However, as if guided by a divine hand, fate intervened.

Suddenly, a taxi arrived! Jessica's face lit up with joy, while Jaclyn exclaimed with excitement, "Taxi! Taxi!" We got into the taxi and upon arriving at Playacar, to our great surprise, it wasn't raining there! The sky was blue, not a cloud in sight, and plenty of sunshine. Incredible! We greeted Mrs. Gordon, and Jessica Lizeth and Jaclyn Elizabeth quickly joined the party. Happily playing with their friends. The party was in a beautiful residential complex with a shared garden with picnic tables. So, I sat down while Mrs. Gordon arranged some food items on the table.

Not even five minutes after our arrival, I heard someone from a distance say, "Hello!" The greeting was in English, and the voice sounded familiar.

Turning towards the sound, I couldn't believe my eyes— it was Roni!... Roni!.... I couldn't believe it was

Roni! Roni was greeting Mrs. Gordon. The rush of surprise and disbelief overwhelmed me. It felt like divine intervention; an answer to my prayers. For some reason, I had to go to Baltimore I thought. This wasn't just a coincidence. It was a miracle! Why? I didn't know. This was God's work, there was no other explanation. (Roni, coincidentally, lived right next to Lolita's house, the birthday girl who was hosting the party). This was incredible! I was so excited that I got a little nervous. I felt my heart pounding strongly. God had brought us exactly to the place and time of the party.

I could have arrived a little later and not seen her, but she came out and greeted Mrs. Gordon just as I arrived. So now I had to gather the courage to ask her for the big favor. It wasn't easy for me, as I really struggled because I had never liked borrowing money. But at the same time, I asked God to give me the strength to do it.

So I gathered my courage and went. I knocked on the door and her son came out. I greeted him and asked, "Is your mom here?" He replied, "Yes, she just went to shower." "Oh, okay," I said, "I'll come back in a little while." So I went back to the party, but I wasn't comfortable anymore, as I was worried about going back.

Some time passed, and I didn't dare to go again. But I thought, "This isn't a coincidence, for some reason, we were invited to the party right next to Roni's house. Roni only came out for a moment and to greet her neighbor, just as I had arrived." All of this was going through my mind. This was undoubtedly the work of God, so I gathered my courage again and went. This time, when I knocked on the door, Roni came out. It was clear that she was very pleased to see me.

"Hello Inés! How are you? It's great to see you again!" she said. Always with her smile and kindness that characterized her. After greeting her, I explained the situation and without hesitation, she responded, "Of course, with pleasure! You know I'm always here to help. Count on it! Tomorrow morning, I'll bring the money to your house." Her words echoed in my mind, almost surreal. My original plan was for the baby to be born in the USA, and then we'd return to Playa after a month. Grateful beyond words, I assured her that upon our return to Playa, I would promptly settle the debt.

Happily, I waited for the party to end and we went home. Bursting with excitement, I exclaimed to the girls, "Guess what? We're going to Baltimore!" Jessica and Jaclyn's faces lit up with delight, eagerly joining me in packing our suitcases. Later, when Denny returned from work, I shared with him the astonishing news of how I had discovered Roni's whereabouts. His disbelief mirrored my own, yet he couldn't contain his happiness at our newfound solution, aligning perfectly with our shared desire for the baby to be born in the United States.

The following morning, as the clock struck ten, a car pulled up outside. Recognizing Roni's vehicle, I dashed down the stairs to greet her. With a warm smile, she greeted me, "Hello Inés, good morning!" However, her cheerful demeanor was tinged with urgency as she explained, "I had a setback and I'm leaving for Cancun, but go to the Gardenias hotel and give this note to the receptionist; he'll give you the money." Handing me a note bearing the hotel's name and her signature, she instructed, "Please, give 300 USD to Mrs. Inés."

It was that day that I found out Roni owned a hotel. With hearts brimming with gratitude, we bid each other farewell excitedly, and I expressed my sincerest thanks as she departed. Undoubtedly life is more fulfilling when you put your trust in God.

I immediately went back up, excited to get the girls and head over to the travel agency for the tickets. Our suitcases were ready for the trip. That day was Christmas Eve, so we had dinner and spent a beautiful Christmas together as a family. And on Friday, December 26th, the girls were very excited about the trip, and I, a little fearful that they wouldn't let me travel. I was wearing a long, loose sweater, a small blanket half-folded over my arm, and my slightly large bag with the intention that my advanced pregnancy wouldn't attract attention, as I was a little afraid because several people had already expressed that they might not let me travel. However, I tried again to put all my trust in God and no one noticed. They didn't even ask me anything. So we headed to the boarding gate to begin our journey to the United States, where our new baby would be born.

Now, dear reader, get ready to board United Airlines flight 1998 and join me in reading the following chapters where you will find the incredible and inspiring stories that made this great event possible.

As we explore the following pages, we will see how each challenge we faced prepared us for the next, and how each obstacle we overcame strengthened us for the path that lay ahead.

Chapter 4

FLIGHT 1998
Journey of Blessings: Mysteries to Uncover

At times, in the course of life, we find ourselves immersed in worries that seem overwhelming, forgetting that we only need to place our faith in God and be grateful for His constant guidance in our lives. With this conviction in our hearts, we continued smoothly towards the boarding gate.

Aware that we had to make a stopover in North Carolina, I was prepared to face the inevitable opinions of others that often accompany our travels. That's life. There are always people who like to keep an eye on others' lives. More often than not, those opinions aren't well-received, as I believe people should worry about their own lives. While we waited to board the second flight, a curious passenger approached with questions about my pregnancy.

"May I ask how far along you are? Are you sure it's safe for you to travel? You seem like you're almost due," she remarked. Maintaining my composure, I responded calmly. "I still have more to go." The lady looked at me incredulously, but ultimately I wasn't concerned because I didn't need her opinions. After all, she wasn't part of the airline; she was just another passenger, so I ignored her. Life teaches us to deal with various situations, and this wouldn't be the exception.

Soon it was time for our next flight, and it didn't hurt to continue taking the same precautions to ensure that everything went smoothly. I was happy that thanks to God, I had sorted out the tickets, and we were on our way. How wonderful it was to feel the joy of life surrounded by my two little daughters during the journey. Both were very entertaining; Jaclyn Elizabeth, due to her young age, was very funny and witty. Jessica Lizeth was a very good and sweet girl. Undoubtedly, both were very intelligent and amusing. I adore them! Each with a unique personality. Jessica Lizeth was very organized and creative, so she invented different games while we were on the flight to make the time pass more quickly and the trip less boring. The time I spent with them was invaluable. They were both lovely. They made me laugh throughout the entire flight. They filled my life with love and joy every moment. They were beautiful, and they still are. They are a great blessing.

Fortunately, we had an excellent flight! At that moment as the plane landed, I felt that life was full of possibilities and that this new baby would bring even more joy to our lives. For each person is unique and incomparable in the essence of their being.

When we disembarked from the plane, it was almost six in the evening. My brother-in-law, Buddy, radiant with joy, was waiting for us at the airport. Jaclyn Elizabeth and Jessica Lizeth were very excited, as Buddy was their favorite uncle. Whenever he had the opportunity, Buddy would entertain and indulge them. He was very cheerful and playful. Always attentive to ensure they didn't lack anything. *More than an uncle, he seemed like a second dad.* As soon as Jessica Lizeth and Jaclyn Elizabeth saw him, they ran to greet him.

Once we had picked up our luggage, we headed to his house. While Buddy drove, the city of Baltimore stretched out before us, with its tall buildings and characteristic bustle. The afternoon sun illuminated the streets as we ventured into this beautiful place. The sound of cars and the murmur of people filled the air, announcing our arrival.

We felt very happy. After hours of travel, we had finally arrived in Baltimore. I looked around, amazed by the vibrant energy of the city. Everything seemed like a dream come true. I had been granted the opportunity to travel to Baltimore so that our baby could be born there. A city that holds very fond memories for me. It's quite different from Playa del Carmen, which with its majestic beaches has a very unique beauty. I felt a bit worried because there was so much to do, but at that moment, the important thing was that we were finally there, thanks to God.

Upon arriving at his apartment, it was almost seven in the evening. We unloaded the suitcases, and Buddy invited us to greet Mrs. Loretta and Mr. Ray, the kind owners of the house. They both welcomed us warmly and offered us something to drink. The girls were given chocolates as a gesture of hospitality. I remember they were m&m's. Mrs. Loretta, upon learning that the purpose of our trip was the birth of the baby, kindly offered to lend me a crib for the days after the delivery, as the plans were to stay a month after the baby was born to avoid exposing him so little to such a long trip on the plane. We said goodbye to Mr. Ray and Mrs. Loretta, thanking them as it had already gotten late and we had to go back to the apartment. We were very tired from the trip, and we needed to rest.

Our plan was for the baby to be born at Franklin Square Hospital since when Jaclyn Elizabeth was born, I had a very positive experience and received excellent care.

The weekend passed, and on Monday, December 29th, I got up very early to call the hospital clinic and make the appointment. The receptionist asked me very kindly, "What insurance do you have?" "None," I replied. "I don't have health insurance." "And when is your baby due?" "In about three weeks," I replied. "Very well," the receptionist said, "let me check... Since your baby's birth is very close, we will make some space to see you today." My eyes lit up with gratitude. "Excellent!" I exclaimed, thankful for her kindness. The appointment was set for ten in the morning. Then my brother-in-law Buddy's promise came to mind. He had offered to support me in whatever I needed because it was Monday, his day off.

When we arrived for the appointment, the receptionist handed me some papers to fill out so they could process the health insurance. "We will call you in a few minutes," she assured me. This reassured and delighted me, as I was a little worried about not having health insurance. However, I knew it wouldn't be an obstacle since we were citizens, and we could process it soon.

After completing the forms, I was directed to an examination room where they performed routine tests on me. The nurse kindly informed me, "We'll also do an ultrasound right away." "That's great," I replied. "Thank you very much." The nurse gave me the necessary instructions and assured me that the specialist would arrive shortly.

While waiting, I took the opportunity to thank God for the existence of that new life inside me and for not having encountered any obstacles to receiving the necessary medical attention at the clinic.

Then the specialist arrived accompanied by the nurse to perform the ultrasound. The doctor took several images, and when she finished, she said, "This machine seems to not be working very well, and I would like to do the ultrasound on a larger machine. Could you come tomorrow?" "Yes, of course," I replied. At that moment, I assumed it was just the machine, and we calmly returned home. We had to wait patiently and come back the next day.

Chapter 5

Tests of Faith: Unexpected News

It was Tuesday, December 30th, the day dawned a bit cloudy and very cold. The air felt different, as if it might snow. Bundled up warmly, we took the girls to their grandmother's house, Mrs. Lillian. She had offered to take care of them while I went to the clinic again. Buddy had to go to work but first dropped me off at the clinic. He worked at the post office, but because it was New Year's Eve, they closed early, so he agreed to pick me up at noon. When I arrived at the clinic, the waiting room was full of people. However, I wasn't worried because I had an appointment, so I didn't have to wait long. A very friendly nurse escorted me to a room.

I never imagined that an ultrasound machine could be that big. The person who would do the ultrasound was there waiting for me. She gave me instructions and a gown to change into. I lay down on the examination table feeling a bit nervous, but it was normal to feel that way. I was in another country, and even though I spoke English, I didn't always understand everything clearly. However, I was calm because in Playa del Carmen I had had an ultrasound and they had told me the baby was fine, so there was nothing to worry about. The doctor, focused on her work, began to move the transducer over my belly.

I watched as she frequently paused and made notes. After a few minutes, the radiologist stopped the ultrasound and had a concerned look on her face. "Please excuse me for a moment," she said before quickly leaving the room. It was at that moment when worry took hold of me. My heart was pounding as I waited, silently squeezing my hands with anxiety.

Please, let my baby be okay, I pleaded with my Heavenly Father with all my might.

The door opened and the radiologist returned with two other doctors. They approached the ultrasound machine and the radiologist showed them the images. Their conversation was hushed, filled with medical terms that I couldn't quite understand. It was at that moment that my anguish and worry intensified. I thought to myself, *Did they find something? What could it possibly be?* I couldn't begin to imagine. I had to remain patient and wait for them to tell me what was happening. Those moments felt like an eternity as I continued to pray fervently that it wasn't anything serious. But I couldn't bear the wait any longer. "Could you please tell me what's going on?" I asked with a worried and slightly trembling voice, barely able to contain my anxiety. The doctor looked at me with compassion and placed a reassuring hand on my shoulder. "Give us a few minutes. We need to review some more details before giving you the results," she responded gently.

Time seemed to stand still as the doctors meticulously examined the images on the screen. Finally, the doctor asked me with concern in her voice, "Is anyone with you?" "No," I replied, "I came alone." "You can get dressed," she said kindly but with a serious tone. "I'll wait for you outside to explain," she added.

I felt my heart pounding and a huge need to cry overwhelming me. At that moment, I had no one beside me to make any comments; all thoughts were within myself. Back then, having a cellphone wasn't as common as it is now, where you can immediately communicate about anything.

With only God to whom I could speak directly, I said, "Give me strength to face whatever comes." I stood up and dressed with trembling hands, my heart pounding heavily. I couldn't imagine what could be happening to my baby. Every second felt like an eternity as I left the ultrasound room, thoughtful and prepared to face whatever would come next.

The doctor was waiting for me outside and gestured for me to enter another room at the end of the hallway. As we walked through the hospital's white corridor, my thoughts were filled with anxiety and anticipation, wondering what news awaited me. We entered a small office, and she said, "Please, have a seat." I tried to stay calm, but my mind was filled with unanswered questions. I was anxious to know, and those minutes felt like an eternity. The silence was overwhelming, broken only by the sound of paper as she flipped through my medical records. Desperate, I asked, "Can you please tell me what's wrong with my baby?" The doctor replied, "The ultrasound results are not very favorable." "What? Why?" I asked again. She said, "Your baby has a very serious heart problem." At that moment, I felt like all the blood drained from my body, and I couldn't hold back the tears. My heart sank in my chest as I listened to her words, trying to maintain composure while processing the gravity of the situation. "We will discuss all the options and develop a plan of action," she said, offering a glimmer of hope amidst the darkness. Desperately, I asked once more, "But what's wrong with my baby? What does he have in his heart?"

I couldn't stop crying. The doctor, concerned, handed me a tissue while trying to comfort me. She waited for me to calm down a bit before explaining. "It's a condition called hypoplastic left heart syndrome. This means the left ventricle didn't fully develop and it has a very important function, as it's responsible for pumping blood to the body. But," she quickly added, "don't cry. There is hope."

"Fortunately, you're in the right place. Here in Baltimore, we have a world-renowned hospital, Johns Hopkins, with an exceptional team of specialists in cardiology, pediatrics, and surgery ready to provide the best care for your baby. I will arrange an appointment as soon as possible so they can attend to you immediately." At that moment, she picked up the phone and began making calls.

When the doctor mentioned that hospital, I felt like a ray of light piercing through my soul, filling me with hope and renewing my faith. As she made the calls to schedule the appointment, tears streamed down my face. Besides the pain I felt from the news, these were tears of gratitude. I thanked God with all my being for guiding me to this moment, for providing the resources to be in the perfect place, and to offer my baby the best possible care.

Amidst the emotions and mixed feelings, I reflected on life's unexpected turns. What would have happened if I hadn't come to Baltimore? Every page of this story seemed to have a divine purpose, and now I understood that every challenge, every obstacle overcome, had prepared me for this crucial moment. I felt like I was exactly where I needed to be, trusting infinitely that God's mercy had led me there to ensure the well-being of my little miracle.

My heart was pounding, not only from the anxiety of the unknown but also from the certainty that we would be in the hands of the best professionals, in a world-renowned hospital. It was a moment of intense emotion, overflowing gratitude, and unwavering faith in the divine power that guides our steps towards the light, even in the most difficult moments of our lives.

I remained in suspense, with these thoughts racing through my mind, while listening to the doctor continue speaking, yet not confirming the appointment. It was the last week of December, and the clinic was closed for the holidays. However, my Heavenly Father was sending angels into my life because my baby's life was at stake.

Fortunately, the doctor managed to reach Doctor Reid Thompson, who despite being on vacation, committed to being the first physician to attend to my baby before and after delivery. I listened as the doctor explained the case to Doctor Thompson, pleading with him to see me as soon as possible, mentioning my distress. After a few tense moments, the doctor excitedly thanked him and confirmed the appointment. I heard her gratefully say, "Thank you! Thank you so much, Doctor Thompson! So, Friday at nine in the morning."

Immediately, the doctor gave me the good news. "You have your appointment," she said. "It's this Friday at 9:00 a.m. at the Outpatient Center of Johns Hopkins Hospital. DoctorThompson is on vacation, but he's going to come specifically to see you." I couldn't believe Doctor Thompson's gesture, willing to help me despite being on vacation—it deeply moved me. What a display of humanity, humility, and professionalism from the doctor.

Tears of gratitude and hope streamed down my face as I thanked God for placing the doctor in my path and for the Doctor's willingness to see me even while on vacation. The doctor, noticing my emotions, comforted me with a glass of apple juice and a warm hug. "Have faith," she said with hopeful assurance, "your baby is going to be okay." I left Franklin Square Hospital immensely thankful for the kind doctor and for Doctor Thompson as well. Amazing people. Angels on my path. There was no other explanation.

When I left the clinic, Buddy was already waiting for me, so on the way, I told him the sad news. But filled with faith and tears in my eyes, I said, "But today more than ever, my faith has to be stronger. They told me there is hope to save his life. They gave me an appointment at a hospital called Johns Hopkins."

Buddy exclaimed, "Johns Hopkins! Yes! It's the number one hospital worldwide! Don't worry, the baby is going to be okay." Once again, I felt a glimmer of hope seeing that there was a way to save my child's life. "When is the appointment?" he asked. "Friday, January 2nd at 9 in the morning," I replied. Buddy, as kind as ever, said to me, "Don't worry, I'll take you. Count on me for anything you need."

From there, we went to Mrs. Lill's house to pick up Jessica Lizeth and Jaclyn Elizabeth. When we arrived at the house, I explained what was happening and started crying again. The girls hugged me, and Jessica Lizeth said, "Don't cry, Mommy. My baby brother is going to be okay. Let's ask God to heal him," Jessica said. "Yes, sweety," I replied. Jaclyn, who was only three years old, with her eyes sparkling like little stars, said to me, "Mommy, I'm going to be a doctor and I'm going to cure my baby brother!" She didn't exactly understand what was going on, but she also looked worried and hugged me.

Mrs. Lill was very cheerful and kind-hearted. She loved making jokes, always trying to make life more fun, and whenever we visited her house, she made sure we were well taken care of.

However, this time she couldn't do it. The news caught us all by surprise, so she was very sad too, and trying to console me about the sad news, she offered me something to drink. Then I asked her permission to use the phone because I needed to talk to Denny, who was still in Playa del Carmen, to explain the situation. Denny, very saddened by the news but trusting that we were in the best place, said to me echoing his brother's words, "Johns Hopkins! Yes! It's the number one hospital worldwide! The baby is going to be okay. Don't worry!"

So every time I heard comments about Johns Hopkins, my life filled with hope and I felt calmer. Later, I called my mom to tell her what was happening. I heard the sadness in her voice when she answered, but immediately she tried to comfort me. "Don't worry, have a lot of faith in God, you'll see that everything will turn out fine."

While listening to my mom's words, tears filled my eyes, and I couldn't hold back the crying. My mom comforted me, saying, "Don't cry, *Reina*," using the term of endearment she always called me, "you'll see that your baby is going to be fine. Nothing is impossible for God. I promise you, I'll start a prayer chain today. Have faith, and you'll see that everything will turn out well." My mom was right. Hearing her comforting words made me reflect.

Have faith. Yes! That was the key. To have faith and wait patiently. So, every day along with my beautiful daughters, we prayed to God for the health of their little brother, eagerly awaiting Friday for the appointment with Doctor Thompson.

We spent New Year's Eve at the house of Mrs. Loretta and Mr. Ray, who kindly invited us to celebrate at their home.

As it was the holiday season, I felt that the days passed by more quickly. The new year began, bringing with it a ray of light and hope. Undoubtedly, *everything was in God's hands.*

Chapter 6

Options, Faith, and Determination

On Friday, January 2nd, as we were on our way to the hospital, Jessica Lizeth, who was very observant, exclaimed, "Look, mommy! It looks like the sky is illuminated!" "How so?" I asked. "Yes, mommy! There's so much light, and today the sky is bluer than other days." "You're right!" I replied. Indeed, she was right. The day was different because since we arrived in Baltimore, every day had been cloudy and rainy. But that day was different. The sun was shining brightly under a deep blue sky. It seemed as if God had lit up the sky to give me a breath of hope.

We arrived, and after all the good things I had heard about the hospital, seeing the building with the name

"Johns Hopkins Outpatient Center" filled me with excitement. It looked majestic to me.

Indeed, the clinic was closed. They opened it just for us that day. Doesn't that seem strange? They opened it just for us. I was anxious to meet with the doctor, for him to explain what the plan would be as the long-awaited day approached.

The building seemed entirely deserted, and upon arrival, a very kind young lady was waiting for us at the door. After introducing herself to us as the doctor's assistant, she led us inside. We took the elevator up to the seventh floor, which housed the Pediatric Cardiology department. Normally in life, you wait for the doctor, but this time was different. Here, Doctor Thompson was already waiting for us and greeted us kindly. "Hello, I'm Reid Thompson," he said. "Please come in." He greeted each of us and asked the girls their names. He offered them to go next door where there was a television and games for children. The girls chose to remain, anxious to learn what Doctor Thompson would say about saving their baby brother. Then we sat down, and he said to me, "First, I'm going to perform an ultrasound to make sure and have a more precise understanding of the baby's situation. Afterward, we'll need to do other routine tests and schedule his birth." "Thank you very much," I replied, still hoping that the other hospital had made a mistake.

But it wasn't the case. When Doctor Thompson finished the ultrasound, he explained to us in more detail the seriousness of the problem. "Hypoplastic Left Heart Syndrome (HLHS) is a medical condition where the left ventricle of the heart does not fully develop before birth. The left ventricle is the part of the heart responsible for pumping oxygenated blood to the body, and this condition causes difficulties in performing its function." As the doctor spoke, everything seemed as if I was dreaming , but that was what my heart longed for - that it would all be just a dream. Yet, it was a reality; that's what was happening.

The doctor continued explaining, "This condition is extremely rare, affecting approximately 1 in every 5,000 to 10,000 babies. It is a very serious condition that necessitates a series of surgeries; otherwise, the baby would not be able to survive. So you have three options," he said to me. "The first would be surgery, which is done in three stages. The baby won't feel any pain because he will always be sedated with pain medications, and as he grows, he won't remember. In this option, the baby will be on a ventilator with oxygen, helping him breathe, and medications will be administered intravenously. There's a seventy-five percent chance of survival with this option, although like everything, it has its risks. The second option is a transplant, but the baby would have to be placed on a waiting list, which is more challenging because the operation would still need to be done while waiting for a donor heart, and finding one for such a small child is very difficult. The third option is to do nothing. Some parents, fearing they won't have the strength to go through the process, prefer to do nothing and let the baby pass away." As he mentioned the last option, my head shook in a gesture of denial, while I thought to myself, *that strength is only gained through faith in God and great love for your child.*

When Doctor Thompson finished explaining the three options, I immediately said, "The first option." With the surgeries, we had a seventy-five percent chance of saving his life, so there was no more to think about. The doctor said to me, "I agree with you, the decision you've made is the best one." "And what would the treatment consist of?" I asked the doctor. "The treatment consists of three stages," he replied, and then continued explaining. "The Norwood is the first stage, which is performed within the first few hours of the baby's life. During this surgery, a new conduit is created to allow oxygenated blood to flow from the heart to the body. Additionally, deoxygenated blood is redirected from the body to the lungs for proper oxygenation. This surgery is crucial for maintaining blood circulation and oxygenation of the body.

The second stage is the Glenn procedure, typically performed when the baby is between four and six months old. During this surgery, the superior vena cava is connected directly to the pulmonary artery. This helps further improve blood flow to the lungs and reduces the workload on the heart.

And the third and final stage, the Fontan procedure, is typically performed when the baby is between two and four years old. During this surgery, the inferior vena cava is connected directly to the pulmonary artery, completing the separation of oxygenated and deoxygenated blood circulation in the heart. This allows deoxygenated blood to flow directly to the lungs, eliminating the need for the heart to pump it.

These three stages of HLHS surgery are crucial as they provide adequate blood circulation, and your baby will have a better quality of life. Moreover, you are in the best place; we have an excellent team of cardiologists. Your baby will be in the best hands."

I was incredibly grateful to the doctor for his excellent care and professionalism. As he finished explaining, I was amazed because it truly was a very serious situation, yet I thanked God for being in the perfect place as he assured me. I felt more at ease knowing once again that there was a ray of hope.

Then, Doctor Thomson gave us instructions for follow-up and to schedule the date for inducing labor. He explained that a series of clinical tests would need to be conducted, and I was to return on Monday. So, once again grateful for all the valuable information, advice, and support, we said goodbye to the doctor.

On Monday, I returned to the clinic for the indicated tests. The nurse explained that there was a connection between congenital heart defects and Down syndrome. She said that while roughly 50 percent of babies with Down syndrome have heart defects, only around 10 percent of babies with heart defects have Down syndrome. One of the tests was to rule out that possibility.

This test is performed by taking a sample of the amniotic fluid surrounding the baby, as it contains cells from the baby that can be analyzed. This procedure is called amniocentesis.

This information was again a surprise to me; although each situation was a challenge that served to strengthen my faith and hold on to it. However, I couldn't hold back the tears. So within myself, I spoke to God and begged Him with all my soul and above all things: "Dear God, I beg you that my baby does not have Down syndrome. Let the results come out negative." And tears streamed down my face. I couldn't stop crying. "Lord, my Father, I leave it in your hands. You have the final word."

The nurse, concerned and moved, gave me a tissue and tried to console me. Then she continued with the explanation of the other routine tests. It was comforting to me that they explained each procedure in detail, as it kept me informed about everything happening with both me and the baby. Upon finishing, before I left, the nurse gave me a card and said: "If you'd like, you can call this number tomorrow to get the results."

So I called Buddy to come pick me up, and while I waited for him, I sat on a bench outside the hospital. I watched as many people came and went, each with their own health concerns, arriving at this place of hope. People from different parts of the world. It was a moment for reflection and gratitude. I thanked God for being one of those people, for giving us the opportunity to be there at Johns Hopkins Hospital. It was a place where technology was at the forefront, where care, understanding, commitment, kindness, professionalism, knowledge, love, intelligence, and eminence made it the best hospital in the world.

Turning my gaze to the sky, I said to my Heavenly Father, "Give me strength, Lord, and strengthen my faith." This became my new motto, a phrase I would repeat constantly.

I knew I had to be strong for my daughters, who were still so young and didn't fully understand many things about life. I had to be strong to give them confidence and security. I couldn't falter. My mission and responsibility were to make their lives happy and to wait for the baby to arrive, to care for him, help him thrive, and give him all the love in the world. I was responsible for strengthening their faith. I had to make them strong, be optimistic, act, and think positively.

And my little baby boy? He was still there inside me, curled up and happy. He didn't know anything. He couldn't even imagine all that he would have to go through to be okay. He wouldn't be in mommy's or daddy's arms when he was born, and his sisters wouldn't be able to hold him, hug him, or dress him either.

We didn't know what was going to happen. All we had left was the most important thing: to continue strengthening our faith, as it was the only thing that would help us face whatever came our way. Besides us, there was our beloved family eagerly awaiting his birth, and together in one heart, we were all in prayer. *Everything was going to be alright.*

Chapter 7

Saint Mary's Grotto: Miracles and Gratitude

When we returned to Mrs. Lillian's house, we were discussing what they had told me at the hospital and the new challenges that would come with the test results. Everything was uncertain at that moment. Tino, a friend of Denny's sister Tina, was visiting, and as we talked about faith in God and the miracles of life, he told us about a sacred place where many miracles had occurred. It was the Grotto at Saint Mary's University.

"If you'd like, I can take you there, tomorrow" Tino kindly offered. "It's about an hour from here." "Yes, yes! I said, "I would love to go. Thank you so much!" I replied excitedly. The girls overheard and Jessica said, "I want to go too, Mommy!" "Of course, sweetheart, we'll all go!" I responded. Jaclyn Elizabeth was playing, and although she was so young, she was very smart and always aware of what was happening around her, so her little voice chimed in, "I want to go too, Mommy!" "Of course, you'll come too." I replied. "Anyone who wants to and can go," said Tino with a smile. Then Buddy said, "If everyone's going, count me in too." So, we all signed up for the trip to the grotto. Excited, Tino agreed to pick us up at nine in the morning.

Next morning, Buddy and I prepared a cooler with juices and some fruits for the journey. On that day, Jessica Lizeth and Jaclyn Elizabeth woke up very early excited for the outing.

Tino picked us up at nine o'clock sharp, just as planned. We quickly placed the cooler in the trunk since everyone was eager to leave.

When we arrived at the Saint Mary's Grotto, to my surprise, right at the entrance was a beautiful image of the Virgin of Guadalupe. There, with all my faith, I asked the Virgin of Guadalupe to perform the miracle—that my baby would be born as healthy as possible and that he would recover well from his surgeries. Knowing about his heart condition and the ongoing tests, I found myself praying fervently about every aspect of his health, including the pending Down syndrome results. In my anxiety and love, I asked for strength to face whatever challenges lay ahead.

We took some photos and then entered. We explored the grottoes and took more pictures. It was a beautiful place. The girls really enjoyed it. I think everybody did. I spent the entire time praying.

When we returned home, I remembered that I was supposed to have called in the morning for the results, but it was already late. Plus, I was a bit afraid to find out, so I decided to wait. So, I waited. And I thought, "I'll call tomorrow."

Since I hadn't called, that same day around seven in the evening, the phone rang. I immediately answered and heard a lady's voice saying, "Hello, I am calling from Johns Hopkins Hospital. Is Mrs. Biedronski available?"

I became very nervous, feeling my hand tremble as I held the receiver. I felt a cold sweat as I waited to hear more, but whatever it was, I knew I had to face it.

"This is she," I said, while silently praying, *Holy Virgin of Guadalupe, please let it be good news.* My mouth felt dry and my heart was paralyzed.

I didn't want to listen, but at the same time, I had to know. My legs were trembling. I was very nervous, but whatever it was, I had to face reality.

Where was my faith? Where was my motto? Sometimes it weakened, and that's when my motto came to my mind and heart. *Give me strength, Lord, and strengthen my faith.*

My racing thoughts were interrupted when I heard her say, "Good afternoon, Mrs. Biedronski. I'm calling to give you the results of the test we did yesterday. We have good news," she said. "The test came back negative for Down syndrome."

Tears welled up uncontrollably, tears of gratitude to God, to the Virgin Mary, to life.

"Thank you so much!" I replied. "Thank you for calling me." I couldn't stop crying tears of joy and gratitude. My prayers had been heard. While I knew we still faced challenges with my baby's heart condition, I felt a wave of relief washed over me. This news gave me hope and strength for the journey ahead.

Thank you, God! A sense of peace settled in my heart. Once again, I felt that spiritual strength within myself and an inner voice telling me, "Never lose faith."

Just then, Jessica Lizeth and Jaclyn Elizabeth came in from playing in the yard. Seeing them, I felt immense emotion. I hugged them and asked, "Would you like to say a prayer for your little brother?" "Yes, mommy!" they replied, brimming with excitement.

When Buddy came, I told him, between happy tears, that the test results had come back negative. With excitement and a satisfied smile, he said, "That visit to the grotto must have had something to do with it." "Absolutely!" I responded. As I got the girls ready for bed, I smiled, *the day had ended with a great blessing*.

Chapter 8

Previous Emotions to the Grand Moment

A week remained until the baby's birth when suddenly, I received a call—it was my sister, Mary Carmen. "Guess what? I'm coming to Baltimore to be with you for the baby's birth!" Her words filled me with immense joy. Knowing she would be with me during such a special moment brought tears of happiness to my eyes.

"How exciting!" I exclaimed enthusiastically. "When do you arrive?" My words overflowed with emotion, eagerly awaiting her response. "On January 14th. I already have my ticket!" Her certainty and love filled me with gratitude. "God willing, I'll be there to help you with anything you need," she said with great excitement and tenderness that moved my heart. She knew that on that day I would have to be admitted to the hospital, and she surprised me by saying she was coming.

The girls were thrilled. "Is Aunt Mary Carmen coming?" they asked excitedly. "Yes!" I said with a big smile. "She's arriving in a week, God willing." "And my daddy?" Jessica Lizeth asked. "When is he coming?" "He's about to arrive," I replied.

Indeed, Denny had told me he would arrive on the fourteenth as well. There was a mix of nervousness and excitement. My mind was flooded with a sea of thoughts.

How I wish my mom could be with me in these important moments of my life, I thought. Only God knows how much I needed her. I missed her so much! I remembered when Jessica Lizeth and Jaclyn Elizabeth were born, how much my precious mom helped me every step of the way. My dear mother was the angel who cared for me even before I was born, who watched me grow and gave me advice throughout my life, who supported me in every moment, but this time she couldn't be there. I needed her so much! However, her moral support was invaluable. I knew that with her soul and heart, she was with me in spirit, and as soon as she could, she would come again.

Similarly, my sisters Maria Esther, Magda, and Lucia, with all their hearts, would have wanted to be with me during those difficult times. Nevertheless, every time we spoke on the phone, their words filled me with hope, optimism, and joy. My brothers Rafael and Salvador, also concerned about the situation, tried to give me all the encouragement they could. The whole family was constantly in prayer.

With their great love, faith, and concern, I felt that even though we were far apart and they couldn't be with me, we were united always in prayer and united in one heart.

During that week, I was organizing and preparing myself for the big day. I was incredibly excited to meet my baby and tell him how much I loved him. But I also felt a mix of fear and hope for his health. Jessica Lizeth and Jaclyn Elizabeth were also getting ready. I told them that I would be in the hospital for a couple of days, but reassured them that they would be fine.

Finally, the long-awaited day arrived. Denny would arrive later that evening, and we planned to meet at the hospital. The girls and I were ready, waiting for Buddy to finish work so we could pick up Aunt Mary Carmen from her friend Cristi's house.

When we arrived at Cristi's house, Mary Carmen came running out to greet us. We hugged and cried tears of joy. Cristi also came out excitedly to greet us. I had been her daughter's teacher back when she was in preschool, and it had been many years since we had seen each other. We were delighted to reconnect after so long. She invited us to spend a few minutes at her home.

Mary Carmen took the opportunity to give me a special gift for the baby that my mom had sent with her. Jessica and Jaclyn were very excited and eagerly helped me open it. The girls were anxious to see what it was. "How beautiful it is!" they both exclaimed. It was a set consisting of striped white and blue-green overall with a matching sweater, perfect for the cold weather in Baltimore. I remember it as if it was yesterday because I was also deeply moved when I saw it. I agreed with the girls. It was beautiful.

Afterward, we went to have dinner at a restaurant before heading to the hospital. It was around seven in the evening, and we went to the home of Conchita, a wonderful friend of several years, from Mexico, a very kind and helpful person. Conchita lived in Fells Point, a beautiful area in downtown Baltimore very close to Johns Hopkins. She would be the one helping to take care of the girls that night, as Mary Carmen would take over the next day.

When we arrived, Conchita was already waiting for us. She was also a person of deep faith in God, always ready to lend a hand. She had prepared some coloring books and a little gift for each of the girls. She invited us to stay, but we had to leave. So we only stayed for a few minutes to make the girls feel comfortable. Then, with a lump in my throat, trying to control my emotions, I said to them, "Everything will be alright. I promise it's just one night that I won't be with you." We said goodbye with hugs, kisses, and smiles. With a heavy heart, I had to leave them. But I left them in good hands. The time for the big event had arrived.

Johns Hopkins Hospital was ten minutes away from Conchita's house, so I also said goodbye to her, thanking her before we left. We arrived at the hospital around nine in the evening. Buddy went to pick up his mom, Mrs. Lillian, because she also wanted to accompany me.

Upon arriving at the hospital, a very friendly nurse greeted us. She led us to the room and explained the procedure for induction and the plan of action after the baby's birth. "The induction procedure can carry risks, as the baby may experience fetal distress. We will proceed as carefully as possible and gradually overnight to minimize these risks," the nurse said. This made me a bit nervous, but I knew I had to trust in God. She then gave me a form to sign authorizing the induction.

She continued, "The surgeon who will perform your baby's surgery is Doctor Mark Redmond. He is an excellent surgeon!" She informed us that the induction process would begin at eleven o'clock at night, aiming for the baby to be born in the early morning hours. This timing was crucial, as the Norwood surgery is a complex procedure performed in several stages and can last for several hours.

"Thank you very much!" I said. As the nurse left the room, my mind and heart were filled with mixed emotions. I felt immense joy knowing that the great moment was just hours away, but at the same time, sadness overwhelmed me as I thought about all that my baby would have to endure to survive, being so tiny. I wouldn't be able to hold him, rock him, shower him with kisses, and tell him how much I loved him.

Mary Carmen seemed to sense my thoughts because she said, "Don't worry. God will work a miracle, and the baby will soon be well." "Yes!" I replied, "you're right!" Silently, I prayed to God for tranquility, peace, and steadfast faith.

Meanwhile, I anxiously awaited Denny's arrival. However, fate had other plans. Denny called to inform me that his flight had been delayed, and he wouldn't make it in time for the birth. My heart sank at the news. We both felt a profound sadness, knowing how desperately he wanted to be present for his son's first moments in the world. Despite the disappointment, I tried to focus on the support I did have around me. Buddy and his mom arrived at the hospital, her presence a comforting reminder that she wanted to be there for me too. Since it was getting late, Buddy left and the three of us Mary Carmen, Mrs. Lill, and I settled into conversation. Before we knew it, it was almost eleven o'clock.

With anxiety, I kept glancing at the clock, and suddenly, just minutes before eleven, I felt the first contraction. With mixed feelings, I exclaimed, "Guess what! I've started having contractions!"

"Really? That's great!" Mary Carmen said with excitement. Denny's mom, always playful, made funny faces that made me laugh. I could tell she was nervous, though. She crossed herself but tried to stay calm. "We need to call the nurse!" she said.

"Don't worry, they've just started," I reassured her with a smile. I knew the arrival of contractions would change the plans, but the confidence that everything would be fine was palpable in every word, as Mary Carmen and Mrs. Lillian were invaluable support, radiating calm and faith amidst uncertainty.

Just as the clock struck eleven, the nurse entered prepared with medications to start the induction process. I exclaimed, "I've started having contractions!"

"Excellent! That's great news," she responded. "I need to inform the doctor." When she returned, she said, "Plans have changed! Doctor Redmond says we should let the natural process take its course because if we induce, the baby would be born around midnight. So, we'll monitor you closely, and when you're close, we'll administer the epidural." They connected me to a monitor to track the contractions.

The intensity of the contractions was just a prelude to what was coming, but even amidst the pain, there was a sense of inner strength that gave me comfort.

By six in the morning, the contractions were very close together and quite strong. I requested the epidural because I felt I couldn't bear the pain any longer. The nurse arrived with the anesthesiologist, and as time passed, the contractions grew closer together. They gave me instructions to sit on the edge of the bed and lean forward slightly. Just as they were about to administer the injection, they asked, "Ready?" "Yes!" I replied, but at that moment, I had another strong contraction. They instructed me to let them know when it passed. "Okay, now!" I said. However, another contraction hit just as they were about to proceed. This cycle repeated several times, but the contractions continued to intensify and draw closer together.

Suddenly, I felt an incredibly strong contraction, as if the baby had dropped right inside me, and I screamed, "The baby is coming! The baby is coming! Don't give me the epidural!"

Mary Carmen and Mrs. Lillian looked on with worried expressions, unable to do anything more than pray for everything to go well. The contractions were so intense that I felt like I was dying.

Soon, the doctor and nurse helped me settle into the bed and quickly wheeled me to the delivery room. Amidst the pain, my screams, and tears, I could only see a flutter of people around me and bright lights.

Mary Carmen and I had planned to take a video of the birth, but due to the chaotic situation, we decided against it. I signaled her not to record. Nevertheless, both of them stayed close to accompany me throughout.

The room was filled with doctors and nurses. It felt like we had entered heaven, and many angels dressed in white were awaiting the arrival of my baby. Suddenly, a sweet cry was heard—it was my son who had just been born!

At that moment, the room filled with a new energy, a reminder of the beauty and fragility of life. Amid tears of joy and excitement, emerged a commitment of love and protection towards my little warrior who was ready to face any challenge that came his way. Ready to fight for his own life!

Then, they placed him on my chest for just a few seconds. With tears of emotion seeing him so beautiful, so defenseless, and so fragile, I gently stroked his head and said, "I adore you, my beautiful boy. Be strong! Be brave! You can do this! God our father will be with you at all times!"

"What will his name be?" a nurse asked me.

"Denny Michael," I replied. In that moment, the chosen name took on a profound new meaning—a declaration of love and strength that would accompany every step of his journey through life. Though the road ahead might be difficult, this name now symbolized our faith in God's presence and care, a guiding light that would lead him through.

With tears in my eyes, I watched as they swiftly took him on a stretcher to prepare for his first surgery. I closed my eyes and spoke to God:

"Father Almighty, in Your hands lies the life of my baby! I know You brought me here to save him! I trust in You,

Lord, and I believe You will work the miracle of his survival. There will come a time when we can hold him, embrace him, see him smile, and tell him how much we love him. Give us strength, Lord, and strengthen our faith."

That moment, filled with hope and unconditional love, marked the beginning of a new adventure, a story of courage and determination destined to inspire all who had the privilege of witnessing it.

Chapter 9

United in Prayer: Awaiting the Miracle

The first hours of Denny Michael's life were critical. Once he was born, they took him to the level IV, regional neonatal intensive care unit (NICU), the highest level of care for newborns. There, they stabilized him and prepared him for his first surgery. After his birth, they took me to my room. About two hours had passed when a kind nurse asked me if I wanted to go see my baby before his operation. Of course I said yes instantly. So, in a wheelchair, they took me to where he was. My little Denny Michael was in an incubator, already connected and ready for his surgery. It broke my heart to see him like that, unable to touch him. Then a young doctor with glasses arrived and introduced himself.

"Mrs. Biedronski?" he asked. "Yes, that's me," I replied.

"Hello, I'm Doctor Mark Redmond," he said. "I'll be the surgeon in charge of Denny Michael's first operation." I was amazed by his youth and the immense responsibility he had on his shoulders. All the world said he was a genius. So my baby was in the best hands.

The doctor explained: "We just ran a test and found a small anomaly that needs to be operated on before the Norwood surgery. So in an hour we are going to perform that surgery, which is risky, but we cannot proceed with the Norwood without addressing this issue first. The baby will be monitored and under the care of two nurses one hundred percent after the surgery."

"And how long will the surgery last?" I asked the doctor. "Approximately 3 to 6 hours," he replied. "Our medical team has conducted a thorough evaluation of the baby and we already have the surgical plan that we believe is most appropriate. The pediatric anesthesiologist is exceptional and he will ensure that the baby receives the appropriate anesthesia to keep him under the entire time, so he does not feel pain. Then we will begin the surgery. We have a lot of faith that he will survive. If everything goes well, we will leave him in recovery for a few days, and in five days we will proceed with the Norwood procedure. In the meantime, I recommend that you rest. A nurse will keep you updated frequently on his progress to help you feel more at ease. We will do everything in our power to save your baby's life." "Thank you very much, Doctor Redmond. We will be praying." The doctor bid farewell.

Meanwhile, I stayed there with my baby, silently speaking to him through the incubator. "Denny Michael, my beautiful boy, you have no idea how much I regret that this is happening to you. I want you to know that I adore you with all my heart. We are all here close to you, praying to God our Father to make you strong and for everything to go well. You need to meet Daddy and your sisters who are eager to come see you. You need to get better so you can meet Uncle Buddy, Aunt Mary Carmen, and Grandma Lill who are out there praying for you. You have to do well. All our family in Mexico can't wait to meet you. They are also praying for you! God brought us here where the best doctors will heal your little heart. I promise you will be fine."

Then the nurses came for the baby to take him to the operating room, and I stayed there with tears in my eyes watching them wheel him away. I closed my eyes and silently said once more, "Give me strength, Lord, and strengthen my faith. My baby's life is in Your hands."

The nurse escorted me back to the room where Mary Carmen and Mrs. Lill were waiting for me. "Guess what?" I said to them, "The baby is already in the operating room" So I told them what Doctor Redmond had informed me, including his recommendation to use this time to rest. Mrs. Lill, who hadn't left since we arrived the night before, decided to go back to her house to rest for a while. We agreed to notify her as soon as we had any news.

"What do you think?" Mary Carmen asked me. "We should also take advantage and rest for a little bit. How does that sound?" "Yes," I replied. "Buddy said he would take his mom home and then pick up the girls at four to bring them to the hospital to spend the afternoon with us. Denny should also be arriving soon. Thank God his flight left earlier this morning, and he told me he'd take a taxi to the hospital as soon as he lands." "Excellent!" Mary Carmen replied.

So we rested for a bit, although not much, as the nurse came in constantly to check on me and update me about the baby's condition. It was almost five in the afternoon when, thank God, Denny arrived. As we embraced, tears streamed down our faces, overwhelmed by a surge of mixed emotions. I felt immense relief and joy at having his support, while he was equally eager to see his son. Just as we were settling into this moment, Dr. Redmond entered the room to inform us about how the surgery had gone and to update us on the baby's condition.

"Everything went well!" he said. "The baby has been transferred to the pediatric intensive care unit for recovery, where he will be closely monitored by the medical team. Now we just have to wait. If the next twelve hours go well, we've made it," he told me. "So keep praying," and with a smile, "keep your fingers crossed." In Mexico, we would say "Haz changuitos."

It seemed incredible to me the excellent care we were receiving. We were very grateful to God and also for all the prayers, as my mom had organized prayer chains and we saw blessings all around. The doctor left, and then Buddy arrived with the girls. They were excited to see us and ran to embrace us. Finally, our little family was all together.

That afternoon, while Denny and his brother were catching up, Jessica Lizeth, Jaclyn Elizabeth, Mary Carmen, and I prayed the Rosary and spent time in constant prayer. Later, I also spoke with my sisters Maria Esther, Lucia, and Magda; they all encouraged me and gave me much hope. Especially Magda, being a nurse herself, reassured me, saying, "Don't worry. Babies are stronger than you think. He will be okay. Have faith". They felt very sad that we were so far away and couldn't be there with us. My mom provided me with a fresh wave of supportive and uplifting words.

The clock ticked away the hours, and with each passing moment, I looked up to the sky, pleading to God to strengthen Denny Michael so that he could survive. The minutes seemed to pass slowly.

Finally, after the twelve hours passed, a collective sigh of relief filled the room when Doctor Redmond returned with hopeful news. "The baby remains stable, which is a very good sign," he announced with a comforting smile. "He will continue in the intensive care unit and receive all the necessary attention for his recovery, which will be crucial for the next surgery." "Thank you, God!

Thank you so much, doctor!" The doctor, very pleased, said, "It's a small step, but a great triumph in the fight for his life."

Knowing that the baby was out of immediate danger for the moment, Mary Carmen and the girls went home with Buddy to rest. While Denny stayed with me, as I hadn't been discharged yet.

The next day, Denny Michael remained stable, thank God. The girls were eager to meet him. "Mommy, when are we going to meet my little brother?" Jessica Lizeth asked. "I want to see him too!" Jaclyn chimed in. So, I spoke with the doctor to see if they could come in, and they said yes. Denny, Buddy, and Mary Carmen hadn't met him yet either, so it was an opportunity for them to come in with me. However, we had to prepare the girls before they were allowed to enter.

Once in the waiting room on the seventh floor, a very kind lady from the Child Life Department arrived with a box of fabric dolls and medical supplies and introduced herself to us. "Hello! I'm Mrs. Joy," she said warmly, addressing the girls, asking for their names. "What's your name?" "I'm Jessica." "And you?" "I'm Jaclyn," they both courteously responded. She gave each of them a doll to care for. They started playing, pretending to be doctors and taking care of the babies. The aim was to prepare them so that seeing their little brother filled with tubes and bandages wouldn't be too shocking.

After half an hour, the nurse arrived and allowed us to enter. Jessica Lizeth and Jaclyn Elizabeth went in, very excited. It was a very emotional moment, seeing our baby there so vulnerable in the fight for life. The girls gently stroked his little arms and told him how much they loved him.

From that moment on, Mrs. Joy developed a deep affection for the girls and took charge of bringing them toys and playing with them the entire time we were at the hospital. She was an incredible person, full of joy and optimism. She always brought something different to keep them entertained and prevent them from getting too tired of being in the hospital. Sometimes she would say to me, "I have some free time, go be with the baby, I'll take care of them." The girls were enchanted with Mrs. Joy, whose name perfectly embodied her character. She was yet another angel in our lives.

Mary Carmen's presence during those difficult moments was invaluable. She always had a desire to give and serve. She was willing to help me with whatever was needed. She enjoyed taking care of her nieces, and when we were at the hospital, we took turns spending time with Denny Michael and attending to the girls.

A couple of days passed, and I was discharged. The greatest longing of a mother giving birth is to leave with her baby in her arms, but this time it was different. I had to leave empty handed. I had to leave my baby at the hospital; I had no other choice. As we left the hospital, tears in my eyes, my gaze lingered on the building where my baby was. In the intensive care unit with several babies, like him, fighting for their lives. What comforted me was that he was surrounded by love and excellent care at the hospital. Without a doubt, God was by his side. And a thought came to mind: *while there is life, there is hope.*

Chapter 10

The Ronald McDonald House

One day before they discharged me, a social worker arrived. "Can I speak with you?" she asked. "Of course," I replied. "I'm Miss Linda, and I need to talk to you about several support avenues the hospital offers for patients who come from out of town or live far away. When you have a moment, come to my office so I can give you all the information and have you fill out some paperwork to expedite the process." She handed me her card and said, "I'll be here until five." "Thank you very much," I responded, taking the card.

Later on, I arrived at her office as instructed. She greeted us very kindly. "We have an incredible family support system at the Ronald McDonald House." "Oh, really? What is it?: I asked. "The Ronald McDonald House is an organization that provides a comprehensive support environment for families with sick children, offering accommodation, meals, emotional support, and other services to assist them during a difficult time." She replied. "Oh, that's great!" I said. "And where is it located?" "It's five minutes from the hospital, they have 24-hour transportation service. You just need to write the time you need to go and return, and how many people will be going." "That sounds great!" I replied. "Thank you so much. What do I need to do to access this support?" I asked. "You just need to fill out these papers, and someone will take you to the Ronald McDonald House for a tour and to meet the staff once you are discharged from the hospital. You'd have your own room with a private bathroom. Each floor has laundry facilities including detergent."

The kitchens are shared on each floor, but each family has their own designated space with their name for storing pantry items in both cabinets and the refrigerator. The prices are very affordable depending on each family's situation. Each family is responsible for keeping their rooms clean, as well as the kitchen and dining area. Everyone is expected to clean up and put dishes in the dishwasher after cooking and eating."

"Excellent! That would be a huge help! It will help us a lot to be closer to the baby."

Everything was arranged that same day. It was a great blessing. The time we spent there was incredible. Families had all the necessary amenities, entertainment, games for children, and much more. Often, different organizations would come on Saturdays and Sundays to support and to cook for all the families, making life easier for us and giving us more time to dedicate to our children.

Chapter 11

Moments of Anguish and Triumph

It was Sunday, January nineteenth. Four days had passed since Denny Michael's birth, and thankfully, he continued to recover from the first surgery. His condition remained stable. A ray of hope began to shine. In the waiting room were Mrs. Lill, Buddy, Denny, Mary Carmen, the girls, and me, taking turns to be with the baby and to care for the girls. Suddenly, we saw Doctor Redmond approaching us.

"I have good news," he said. "Denny Michael has responded exceptionally well. We are ready." He kindly explained the next steps. "We need you to sign the authorization for us to proceed tomorrow morning with the Norwood surgery. We will start at six-thirty as it is a procedure that may take several hours. A member of the medical team will keep you informed of progress." "Thank you very much, doctor," I replied.

Although we had already been briefed on the procedure for each surgery, the doctor emphasized the importance of reviewing the details before signing the authorization. I nodded gratefully, fully aware of the responsibility involved. It was our baby's life at stake, and we had to trust Doctor Redmond, the medical team, and above all, God, as our son's life was in their hands.

Then, the doctor continued to explain: "The Norwood operation is a complex surgical procedure used to treat hypoplasia of the left heart. This intervention will take approximately four to six hours. If all goes well and no complications arise, I don't expect it to last longer. Nevertheless, a member of our team will be responsible for keeping you informed regularly."

"Thank you very much, doctor," I replied again.

We returned to the Ronald McDonald House, and I signed up for the van to pick us up early in the morning to arrive at the hospital before the surgery. At five-thirty in the morning, we were ready to go to the hospital. Mary Carmen stayed with the girls, and they would join us at the hospital later.

So, Denny and I arrived and went straight to the intensive care unit where our precious child was. Each time we arrived, the nurses would greet us with a box of tissues, aware of how emotionally difficult those moments were for us. However, amidst tears and words of encouragement, I found the necessary strength to face the situation.

Gently stroking his fragile head, I spoke to him with love and determination. "You're a champion! You've passed the first test, *mi rey*! God is with you. You have to be strong, my beautiful boy, you can do it! We want to see you open your eyes and see you smile," I spoke to him, pouring out all of my maternal faith and love. With a blessing and a prayer, we accompanied him to the operating room door, entrusting his life to divine hands and the skill of the medical team.

In the waiting room, surrounded by silent prayer, we found comfort in the company of Mary Carmen and my two beautiful daughters. Together, we immersed ourselves in spirituality, praying the rosary and asking the Virgin to watch over Denny Michael. Although young, the girls participated devoutly, their innocent faith serving as a beacon of hope amidst the darkness.

Time seemed to pass slowly, but our faith remained unshakeable. Between prayers, stories, and games, we found solace in routine and in the kindness of the medical team, whose constant care and compassion comforted us in our most difficult moments.

Around one o'clock in the afternoon, the doctor emerged with good news. "Everything went very well," he announced, filling us with relief and gratitude. Every minute gained was a step closer to hope, and every word of encouragement was a reminder of the power of such great faith and unconditional love. Later that afternoon, Pastor Ramirez visited us, a friend from the church who kindly prayed with us.

It had been a few days and everything was going well, when suddenly, Denny Michael gave us the scare of our lives! His heart rate shot up to 200 beats per minute; his condition became extremely critical. The monitors' alarms started blaring! The incredible medical team seemed to appear out of nowhere, instantly filling the room with doctors and nurses to stabilize the situation that seemed too critical. I was cautious and immediately stepped out not to interfere, as is customary during procedures. It was a moment of intense anguish. My heart was pounding heavily. I couldn't stop the tears from flowing. Mary Carmen encouraged me with her words and held me in her embrace. And my sweet girls had incredible faith. When she saw me crying, Jessica Lizeth said, "Let's pray, I have the rosary." Jaclyn Elizabeth quickly joined in and began reciting the Hail Mary.

It took approximately an hour for them to stabilize him. During that time, a nurse would often emerge to give us words of encouragement. Finally, thanks to God, they succeeded. It was yet another triumph! The doctors and nurses said that at several moments they felt the situation was slipping out of their hands, but

"Denny Michael clung to life." Undoubtedly, it was a miracle! There was no other explanation.

Chapter 12

Overcoming Obstacles:
With Faith, Everything is Possible

A month had already passed. It was a very difficult month since Denny had to be absent due to a crisis that led him to be hospitalized in another hospital for several weeks - a story for another time. The situation became somewhat challenging for me as I sometimes had to alternate between hospitals, but thanks to the great support of my sister, things became a bit easier. However, all things come to an end. My sister Mary Carmen had to return to Mexico. Jessica Lizeth and Jaclyn Elizabeth were very sad, and with a heavy heart, we said goodbye to her. I will be eternally grateful for her tremendous support. Later on, without Mary Carmen's support, we decided to leave the Ronald

McDonald House and only return on weekends so that Jessica Lizeth could continue attending school.

We found a lovely daycare for Jaclyn Elizabeth that offered both educational activities and childcare services. Now, the challenge was to find a way to visit my baby while they were at school. Denny had already been discharged from the hospital and could help me a little as well. Buddy had Mondays off and offered to drive me to the hospital, but for the rest of the week, I wasn't sure how to get to the hospital since Buddy lived quite far away. We needed to find a solution, and I trusted that God would guide me. So, I began to do some research.

The "Light Rail" was a train that took me downtown, from where I could take the metro that would drop me right at one of the entrances to Johns Hopkins. The question was: How to get to the Light Rail? For the time being, Buddy took me on Mondays. On Tuesdays, while the girls were at school, I spent the day crying in sadness for not being able to visit Denny Michael. Even though it wasn't true, I felt like I had abandoned him! I prayed to my Heavenly Father with all my faith, asking him to somehow provide the means for me to visit my son, even if only for a little while every day. I knew that my presence and being there for him were crucial to his recovery. On those days, I could only call to check on him. There had to be a solution, so I began to investigate.

Taking a taxi from home to the Light Rail was too expensive, so I discarded that option. The possibility of taking a public bus was only viable on Ritchie Highway, but it was a bit far away. To get there, I would have to walk about three miles, but no matter how much I thought about it, that seemed to be my only alternative.

It would take me two hours to get to the hospital, but that didn't matter. The important thing was to get there somehow. Denny would take care of Jaclyn Elizabeth, and I would take Jessica Lizeth to the school bus stop. Once she left, I would walk to the bus stop and, on my return, Buddy would pick me up at the Light Rail station. God had enlightened me. It was a complete plan.

The next morning, Jessica Lizeth and I were waiting for the school bus when I noticed a parked car. Inside, a girl and her mom were also waiting for the bus. I said goodbye to Jessica Lizeth and saw the girl was also bidding farewell to her mom. I approached the car and greeted them. The mother kindly responded to my greeting. I asked if by chance she would pass by Ritchie Highway, and she responded with a question: : "Where are you going?" So, I explained the situation. "I have my baby in the hospital, and while the girls are at school, I want to go see him. I just need to catch a bus on Ritchie Highway that takes me to the Light Rail, and from there, I'll take the metro to Johns Hopkins."

Smiling, the lady replied, "Actually, I pass by the Light Rail every day on my way to work. If you'd like, I can drop you off there whenever you need." "Thank you so much!" I responded with deep gratitude. It was incredible! I was amazed! Undoubtedly, it was the work of God. I could feel it! There was no other explanation. Truly, she was another angel in my path. She was so kind that the next day, when I got into her car, she had a gift for Denny Michael.

With this great help of being dropped off at the Light Rail station, I could spend the entire morning with Denny Michael and return early to attend to the girls in the afternoon.

Days passed and Denny Michael appeared more recovered. After two months, one day we were all at the hospital and the nurse asked us, "Would you like to hold him?" "Yes, of course!" I replied. Soon they brought a rocking chair and helped me arrange all the wires so I could hold him. That day, Denny was also happy that he could hold him too. His little sisters also got to see him, even if only for a little while. It was an unforgettable day!

The next day, Doctor Redmond spoke with me: "We've seen a lot of improvement in Denny Michael, and we've decided it's time to remove the oxygen ventilator. If he manages to breathe on his own, we can discharge him and send him home." "That's great! How exciting!" I exclaimed, feeling an overwhelming urge to cry from sheer happiness. "This is excellent news," I said excitedly. The doctor smiled with satisfaction, pleased with the progress of his little patient. "We'll try first thing tomorrow morning," he added.

The next morning, they attempted but unfortunately, he didn't pass the test. So the doctor told me, "Don't worry, we'll try again in two days. We just need to give him a little more time." Two days later, the second attempt was also unsuccessful. So the doctor said, "We can't give up! Let's make a third attempt."

They tried a third time and still, it wasn't successful. The doctor said, "We thought he would make it, as he's very close to where we want him to be."

I felt very sad and discouraged, but I stayed in constant prayer. I approached Denny Michael and gently stroked his head, saying, "You can do it, baby! You're a champion! God our Father will give you the strength you need, and you will achieve it, my sweet boy!"

At that moment, another doctor arrived and asked to speak with me. She explained that typically, three attempts are made, and if babies do not respond, the next step is a tracheostomy. "And what is that?" I asked. The doctor kindly explained, "A tracheostomy is a surgical procedure where an opening is created through the neck into the windpipe to assist with breathing. It is performed in very extreme cases in babies." She then took me to see another baby who had undergone this procedure. I couldn't help but shed tears once again.

The doctor, seeing me so distressed, said, "We believe Denny Michael is on the verge of being able to breathe on his own, but we want you to be prepared in case he doesn't." "Yes, doctor, I understand," I replied. So Doctor Redmond and the medical team decided to give him another chance.

Immediately, I called my mom and told her the situation. "You know, Mom," I said, "I'm very sad because there's a possibility that Denny Michael will have to have a tracheostomy. They've tried several times to remove the oxygen ventilator, and he still can't breathe on his own."

My mom, being a nurse herself, understood perfectly well what was going on and what a tracheostomy entailed. "Don't worry, Reina," she said. "Right now, I'm going to start another prayer chain so that it won't be necessary. You'll see he won't need it. Have a lot of faith!".

So the days went by. All the nurses greeted us kindly and encouraged us. "He has to make it," they said with conviction. This was the fourth attempt. Sadly, once again he didn't succeed. I couldn't hold back my tears, as the doctor had already told me that if he didn't make it this time, the next step would be a tracheostomy.

Then Doctor Redmond approached me and said, "Normally, we never go beyond three attempts, but Denny Michael is so close for us to give him a tracheostomy. We believe he can do it. Our plan is to give him one more week, and we'll try for the fifth time. We have faith that he will succeed."

Grateful, I expressed my thanks to them. I called my mom and said, "You know what, Mom? They're giving him a fifth chance." My mom was very happy to hear that. "We're still here in prayer!" she told me.

The day arrived, and Doctor Redmond said to me, "Today is the big day, keep your fingers crossed. This time we're going to make it," he said with great certainty. "In God's hands." I replied. "As always, we will keep you informed," he concluded.

So we waited patiently in the waiting room near where Denny Michael was, in constant prayer because this time it was the final attempt. If he succeeded, he wouldn't need the tracheostomy, which was what we all desired.

Suddenly, we heard all the nurses and doctors applauding! The applause was for Denny Michael. They called me over and congratulated us. The girls, Denny, Buddy, and I were overjoyed! Everyone was in tears, even the nurses were crying tears of joy. I couldn't stop thanking God and sending blessings to my mom and everyone who had been praying for him.

This meant that Denny Michael was being discharged. We could finally take him home, though he would still need a small oxygen tank to assist him while he continued to regain strength, along with a feeding tube. But it was manageable. Moreover, during my time there, I had learned a lot. We received training and took a CPR class. Now, we would patiently await the next surgery, the Glenn procedure, scheduled for when he turned six months old.

I was extremely excited and called everyone to share the good news and thank them for their prayers. I called my mom, my siblings, Mary Carmen, Mrs. Lill, and Conchita. "He did it! Thank you for your prayers!" I also thanked God and the Virgin Mary for being with Denny Michael and us through every step of the way. Although there was still a long way to go, we just had to continue feeding our faith and trusting in God's infinite mercy.

When we went to see him, we said, "Bravo, Denny Michael! You are a champion! You are a warrior! You did it!" And as if he understood everything we were saying, Denny Michael gave us a little smile.

Chapter 13

Triumphs and Preparations

His first six months of life were marked by countless achievements and a beautiful transformation for all of us. My two little daughters became involved in caring for their baby brother in an extraordinary way. Finally, without the help of the oxygen ventilator, we could delight in his babbling, laughter, and cries. Despite his young age, Denny Michael showed a radiant personality, brimming with joy and smiles. Every gesture seemed to be a thanksgiving to life and to all the people who had prayed for him. Thank God, his recovery process was amazing! We could not have gone through this stage without the most dedicated care and attention.

Once we left the hospital, Doctor Thompson continued as his pediatric cardiologist, and I must pay tribute to his exceptionalism, as well as to the pediatric cardiology team at the John Hopkins Outpatient Center. From the first encounter, I was impressed by his commitment, love, and humanism. He was truly amazing!

With a heart full of gratitude and hope, our little warrior triumphantly entered the second stage of his treatment at six months old. Doctor Redmond, once again, kindly explained the details of the new procedure to me:

"The second stage of the surgery, as you know, is the Glenn procedure. It is essential as it improves blood circulation to the heart and lungs. I will create a connection between the superior vena cava and the pulmonary artery, allowing blood to flow directly from the upper body to the lungs, bypassing the right atrium of the heart. This surgery will significantly improve Denny Michael's quality of life and his ability to engage in daily activities. However, it is crucial that he continues to be closely monitored by the medical team". I nodded and thanked him once again.

"We are ready," said Doctor Redmond. "Now they will take Denny Michael to the operating room, and one of our nurses will be responsible for giving you constant updates on how we are doing." Grateful to the doctor, I made my way to the waiting room with a calmer heart. The light of the new day filtered through the hospital curtains, and I felt thankful to God, knowing that my son was in the best hands. Furthermore, we were very happy because this time my beautiful mom was with us, offering her unconditional support as always.

It was six hours of waiting and considerable anxiety, as every surgery carries risks, and this one was no exception. But thanks to God, everything went well. Doctor Redmond personally came to us after the surgery, looking very satisfied, to tell us that everything had gone smoothly. Now, we just had to wait for the recovery.

A few days later, doctors noticed that Denny Michael wasn't moving his left hand and foot normally. They asked if I had noticed anything, but I hadn't. Tests revealed these were side effects sometimes caused by medications and anesthesia. He needed a plaster cast on his hand and, with time and therapy, he began to recover—though not completely.

The next challenge was helping Denny Michael to eat on his own. Due to the long time he had been tube-fed, he rejected any food and even water, so he continued to rely on the gastrointestinal tube for nourishment.

First, we managed to get him to drink water, but he refused everything else. One day, my friend Conchita suggested trying to feed him with a syringe, a method she had used with her own child in a similar situation. At first, I was scared because he seemed disgusted and choked.

Jaclyn Elizabeth, always attentive to how to help her little brother, wanted to give it a try. Surprisingly, Denny Michael accepted the food when she used the syringe. Thus, Jaclyn became my helper in feeding him this way.

When I consulted Doctor Thompson about this method, which other doctors did not recommend, he said, "You're his mom. If you feel it's right, keep doing it." From that moment on, Denny Michael gradually continued to improve his eating.

At 18 months, we returned to Playa del Carmen. Denny Michael still wasn't eating enough, so we went back with his gastrointestinal device. One day it accidentally came out, and the doctor advised not to reinsert it, hoping it would close on its own within a week. But after three weeks of much suffering and no closure, I decided: No more! I won't allow my baby to keep suffering.

I returned to Baltimore, where we were seen at the hospital right away. Denny Michael required surgery, but the day after the operation, he became the happiest child in the world. Thank God he never had eating problems again. Jessica Lizeth and Jaclyn Elizabeth played a major role in this recovery. They were always helping with his therapies. And my mom, being a nurse, was undoubtedly a great support as well. She took extended leaves of absence from work to be able to assist me with the necessary care.

Denny Michael soon recovered and grew up healthy and strong, bringing us much joy, as he was a very clever, kind, and cheerful child.

On the other hand, sadly for Denny, it was very difficult for him to face everything we were going through, so we had to decide what was best for the children, and we chose to take different paths. He stayed to live in the United States while I returned with the children to Mexico. However, he always loved the children dearly and continued to be a part of their lives throughout his life.

When Denny Michael was three years old, we returned to Baltimore for the final surgical stage, which was the Fontan procedure. This time, Doctor Redmond was no longer his surgeon, as he had returned to Dublin, his hometown. Instead, Doctor Duke Cameron performed the surgery, who is also an expert in pediatric cardiology. Just like Doctor Redmond, he came to the waiting room and introduced himself very kindly.

"I am Doctor Cameron. I will be in charge of your son's surgery today. As you should already know, the Fontan procedure is the final stage of the treatment. During this surgery, we will connect the inferior vena cava directly to the pulmonary artery, thus completing the separation of oxygenated and deoxygenated blood in the heart, allowing the right ventricle to perform the function of both. This will allow the right ventricle to perform the function of both, enabling deoxygenated blood to flow directly to the lungs without the heart needing to pump it, thus improving Denny Michael's quality of life."

I greatly appreciated how they always took the time to explain in detail what they were going to do and what each surgery or procedure involved. Therefore, Doctor Cameron's words gave me encouragement and confidence that everything would go well. Now, all we had to do was wait again with faith and patience.

The surgery was expected to last approximately four to six hours. So, my mom, Jessica Lizeth, Jaclyn Elizabeth, and I gathered to pray and patiently await the results. We were also joined by Conchita, Buddy, Mrs. Lill, as well as our dear Cathy and Mike Davis, true friends from church who were always attentive and ready to support us. All united in prayer, waiting patiently together.

Thankfully, once again, Denny Michael emerged triumphant, though a bit resentful towards mom. When he came out of surgery, he was angry with me. Approaching his bed, I noticed he had his face turned to the side, with a serious expression, and didn't want to look at me. Initially, we thought it might be lingering effects of the anesthesia, but the doctor reassured us that everything was fine. Perhaps upon waking up and not seeing me, he felt a bit disappointed and maybe abandoned, as there was no one familiar around at that moment. Even though the medical team was excellent and treated him with much affection, he didn't like waking up without seeing mom or his little sisters. That's why he was so upset.

My poor Denny Michael, my great warrior, so small - he was only three years old - if only he knew how deeply I wished he never had to go through all of that. Seeing him like that broke my heart because my innocent child couldn't fully understand what was happening around him. Despite my attempts to explain before the surgery, his young age limited his comprehension of the seriousness of the situation. Jessica Lizeth and Jaclyn Elizabeth, a bit older and more aware of the situation, were also very concerned about their little brother's unexpected behavior. So they found ways to make him smile. Jessica Lizeth brought him a teddy bear and Jaclyn Elizabeth made him a card with stickers. Seeing his sisters, Denny Michael couldn't resist and soon gave us a smile, as his sisters meant the world to him. Gradually, his mood lifted, and he welcomed our hugs and kisses with open arms.

Jessica Lizeth was a cheerful, detail-oriented, and very creative girl. A true artist. She was always making beautiful and meticulously detailed drawings. Jaclyn Elizabeth was also very cheerful and humorous. She always sought ways to entertain her little brother and help him in every possible way, demonstrating a spirit of cooperation and great sensitivity.

Thank God, everything turned out as we hoped, and soon we were able to return to Mexico to continue with a normal life. Of course, this involved continuing his care, medications, and making visits every six months to the United States for follow-up with his pediatric cardiologist.

Denny Michael remained stable and grew up healthy and happy, always with the constant support of his sisters, who acted like two more little moms, always looking out for him. Undoubtedly, they were and have been two more angels throughout Denny Michael's life. From the moment they first learned about his heart condition, they were focused on praying for him and supporting him in every way.

And I am constantly giving thanks to God for His divine hand in every moment. Because without a doubt, Denny Michael is *a miracle of life.*

Chapter 14

A Miracle of Faith: The Power of Prayer

When Denny Michael was nine years old, I made the decision to return to live in the United States, this time to Tampa, Florida. The reason was clear: it greatly facilitated the continuation of his treatment. We were recommended to the *All Children's Hospital* in Saint Petersburg, now affiliated with Johns Hopkins, where he has received top-quality cardiology care to this day. This hospital, like Johns Hopkins, has highly skilled and professional staff.

We will always miss Doctor Thompson, but when we moved to Tampa, there was no longer a need to go all the way to Baltimore, as we were blessed to have Doctor Alfred Asante-Korang as his new pediatric cardiologist for several years. He, along with his entire medical team, provided us with incredible care.

Since Denny Michael was born, the possibility of a heart transplant had been discussed. However, thanks to the surgeries and excellent medical treatment he received, it had not been necessary to consider it. Denny Michael continued with his appointments every six months, undergoing regular medical tests. For several years, thankfully, he had not experienced any complications.

One day, when Denny Michael was sixteen years old, we arrived for his appointment with Doctor Asante-Korang. Kindly, he ushered us into his office and gave us some not-so-good news: "I believe it's time to consider a heart transplant for Denny Michael." Surprised, I asked, "Why?"

The doctor, with concern, very kindly and in detail explained to us that the results of the latest study revealed a delicate issue with Denny Michael's blood circulation. His liver was in decline, showing signs of possible cirrhosis. This posed a significant challenge because, if the heart transplant was not performed, his other organs could also be at risk and need transplants. This would greatly endanger Denny Michael's life. The news was not the most encouraging, and immediately all the preparations began to include Denny Michael on the waiting list to proceed with the transplant. This meant his hospitalization, as there would be no time to lose when a donor was found.

At sixteen years old, Denny Michael was more aware of the risks involved. Jessica Lizeth and Jaclyn Elizabeth, though very saddened, showed incredible maturity and were willing to offer him all their support. For me, the situation was devastating, as it meant facing numerous risks once again. However, it was crucial to maintain optimism and remember that for God, nothing is impossible. Everything would turn out fine.

One night at the hospital, while Denny Michael slept, I decided to watch a documentary about heart transplants. It was not easy. Tears streamed down my cheeks as I imagined my son going through something similar. After it ended, with Denny Michael still sound asleep, I kissed him on the forehead, entrusting him to God and to the Virgin of Guadalupe. With the late hour, close to two in the morning, the hospital corridors were deserted, so I was not concerned about anyone seeing me cry. I felt overwhelmed with sadness and couldn't contain my tears. I entered the chapel, knelt down, and pleaded with God that they wouldn't have to subject Denny Michael to a transplant, asking for another solution. I cried and cried, pouring out my anguish.

When I returned to the Ronald McDonald House where I was staying, I went to my room. In the silence of the night, sitting on my bed, I once again spoke to God, begging for a miracle to avoid the transplant. Finally, I fell asleep. Upon waking early, my first thought was again to speak earnestly with God: "Please, Father, shed light on the medical team to find another solution." All I could do was trust in Him. I quickly got ready and returned to the hospital.

Despite my sadness and distress, I tried not to show it in front of Denny Michael so he could feel calm; I wanted to convey peace and encouragement to him. But he sensed it anyway. With a hopeful smile on his face, he said, "Mom, everything is going to be okay. Don't worry." We spent the day together, praying, playing, laughing, and watching movies while we awaited news.

We had been in the hospital for several weeks when they performed a procedure to map his veins in preparation for the transplant. The team of cardiologists was deliberating on what would be best for Denny Michael. Finally, Doctor Asante-Korang arrived to inform us that during that study they had found a calcified clot in the part of the vena cava that carries blood to the liver. Given this new finding, they were considering either the transplant or another surgery. The alternative, if successful, could reduce the likelihood of a transplant to 30 percent.

Days passed, and the anxiety grew. With each open-heart surgery Denny Michael had endured in childhood, the risks of another operation increased.

Once again, I asked God to avoid the surgery and for them to find another solution.

After a long wait, Doctor Asante-Korang finally arrived with news of a less invasive procedure. Doctor Cameron, who had performed the surgery 13 years ago, reviewed Denny Michael's case again and after conducting a study with the medical team, they decided to perform only a catheterization and place a double stent to fix the blood flow issue to the liver. The plan would be to monitor, and if the liver began to respond positively, it wouldn't be necessary to proceed with either surgery for the time being. A feeling of relief and gratitude filled the room. God had heard our prayers! "It's a miracle, Denny Michael! It's a miracle!" I exclaimed.

Feeling the divine presence that had guided every step of our journey, tears of gratitude streamed down my face. Undoubtedly, God had heard us and granted us yet another miracle, and now we had to continue praying, trusting that this new treatment would be the solution.

It has been ten years now, and I am eternally grateful that Denny Michael has not needed any more surgeries and that a transplant has not been necessary so far. It is evident that God led us to the most skilled hands of incredible human beings, so I want to take this opportunity to give special recognition to Dr. Reid Thompson, Dr. Mark Redmond, Dr. Duke Cameron, and Dr. Alfred Asante-Korang—excellent doctors who gave their all: knowledge, time, dedication, passion, and love. I also extend my gratitude to the entire medical team who was and has been involved in every surgery and every step of Denny Michael's treatment journey, both at Johns Hopkins in Baltimore and at All Children's in Saint Petersburg.

Each of you has been an invaluable piece in this journey towards my son's recovery.

I would like to express my deepest gratitude to Mike and Cathy Davis, dear friends from the Evangelical Presbyterian Church in Baltimore. Their constant support and generosity were invaluable to us. I consider them true angels sent by God to accompany us on this difficult journey, as their moral support was indispensable at all times.

Furthermore, thanks to them, we had the fortune of meeting Pastor John Keen, Pastor Danny Dalton, and our church family from Christ Central Presbyterian Church. Upon arriving in Tampa, they also provided us with incredible support, which allowed us to continue

Denny Michael's treatment. Their spiritual support, help, and kindness made a significant difference in Denny Michael's life and to ours, for that, we are eternally grateful.

Similarly, I want to express my deepest gratitude for the unwavering support and sincere prayers from my beautiful family, our friends, and all those who stood with us at every moment. To every angel who crossed our path. Your positive thoughts and energy have been a constant source of strength for us.

I also want to express deep gratitude to Mary Carmen for her kindness and unconditional support during the most difficult moments, especially for her invaluable help before and after Denny Michael's birth. Her presence and support were fundamental both in the hospital and at the Ronald McDonald House. And I cannot fail to mention Buddy, my brother-in-law, whose generosity and unwavering support have been like a beacon in my children's lives. He has always been by our side, in moments of joy and in the toughest challenges. For them, he has been more than an uncle; he has been like a second father.

I cannot thank my two beautiful daughters enough, Jessica Lizeth and Jaclyn Elizabeth, who have been with us every step of the way providing their support since they were very young. Their joy and optimism were incredible and the strengthening source of my faith. Thanks to God, they have grown up maintaining their virtues and special qualities, becoming exceptional women who continue to inspire those around them with their creativity, intelligence, and generosity.

To the staff and co-founders of the Ronald McDonald House, and to all the families who have supported not just my own family, but hundreds of children and families throughout our journey, I extend my heartfelt gratitude.

And, especially, my deepest gratitude to God, for His constant guidance and for strengthening our faith at all times. It is because of this trust that we have been able to face each challenge with courage, and it is through this faith that Denny Michael has truly become a miracle of life.

Life Anecdotes

When we finally returned to Playa del Carmen, a year and a half into Denny Michael's life, I had been meaning to find Roni, as I knew I owed her. I set out to locate her to settle that debt. So, I went searching, but to my surprise, I learned that the hotel was no longer hers and that she had returned to the United States. This news left me extremely sad, as I had no way to contact her.

One day, while Jessica and Jaclyn were at school, I had to do some shopping at Sam's Club and took Denny Michael with me. While in line to pay, Denny Michael slipped away and ran to the other end of the checkout lanes. I called out to him, "Denny Michael! Denny Michael!" but he kept running, so I left my things and ran after him. I called out to him again, but it seemed as if he couldn't hear me. To my surprise, I saw him running towards a woman who was opening her arms towards him. "Roni?" Yes! It was Roni! I was surprised to see her, and she was surprised to see me too.

"Don't tell me it's him."

"Yes, it's Denny Michael," I replied. We hugged, both of us in tears. I apologized for not returning sooner, but she kindly reassured me not to worry about the debt, saying that seeing Denny Michael was enough for her.

To this day, I consider it all a miracle. Roni was an angel in my path, and Denny Michael, with his childlike wisdom, knew she was the angel sent by God to make our journey to the United States possible. That's why he ran to hug her and thank her.

One day, when Denny Michael was around three and a half years old, I was washing dishes in the kitchen and the girls were busy with their tasks. Denny Michael came in, "Mommy, let's play!" he said enthusiastically. "In a little while, *mi rey*," I responded, "let me finish washing the dishes." Then, in a tender tone, he asked me, "When are you going to stop working so much, mommy?" I jokingly replied, "The day a prince comes and takes me to his castle. Then I won't have to work anymore."

Denny Michael paused for a moment, deep in thought, and then went off to play—or so I thought. I continued tidying up the kitchen when suddenly I heard a knock on the door. "Who is it?" I asked. To my surprise, a beautiful voice replied, "It is your prince." I opened the door, and there was my little prince.

On another occasion, as we were walking back home, I asked the kids what they wanted to be when they grew up. Jessica said, "I want to be a ballerina," and Jaclyn replied, "I want to be a doctor!" When it was Denny Michael's turn, he said with determination, "I want to be a dad." I asked, "A dad? How many children do you want to have, *mi rey?*" With a charming smile, he replied, "Two boys, because we already have two girls." It was very funny and witty of him. He knew there were already two girls in the house, so now he thought we needed two boys. He was always a cheerful and fun-loving boy, with a contagious laugh that brightened our lives.

Over the years, Denny Michael enjoyed many passions. From playing with Legos to taking on the role of "dad" in his sisters' games, his creativity and energy were boundless. But what he enjoyed most was watching movies, especially those that allowed him to immerse himself in magical and fantastical worlds. His favorite movie was "Harry Potter," a passion he has carried with him to this day. An unforgettable experience for him was visiting the "Wizarding World of Harry Potter" at Universal Studios, where he was selected from among a large crowd of eager fans to take part in an exciting show at Ollivander's Wand Shop.

Beads of Courage

Each bead represents a surgery or procedure that Denny Michael has undergone since birth and throughout his life journey, not counting the last ten years. The six hearts symbolize each open-heart surgery.

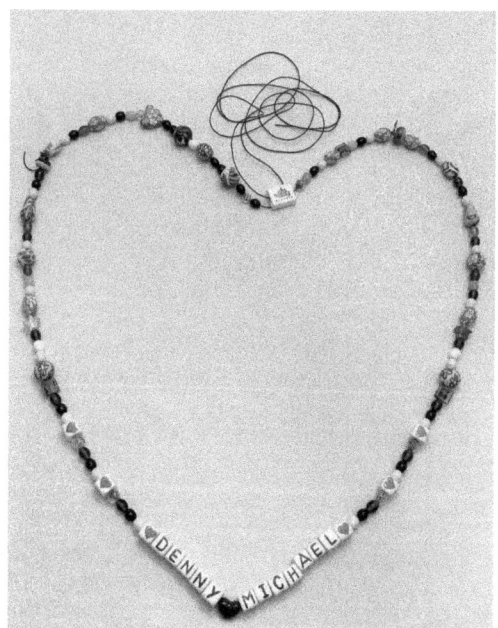

Successes and Recognitions

Denny Michael was always a beloved child by his teachers and classmates, known for his kindness and nobility. His exemplary character was recognized when he received the prestigious "Timothy Award" at his school for being an example in word, conduct, love, spirit, faith, and purity.

In February 2018, Denny Michael started his own YouTube channel which bears his name, and he discovered his passion for music. Since then, he has captivated everyone with his beautiful voice and talent. With every cover he performs, he continues to showcase the special gift that God has bestowed upon him.

In May 2021, Denny Michael graduated from Hillsborough Community College, receiving his Associate in Arts diploma. This degree is awarded upon completion of and compliance with the necessary educational requirements in humanities, social sciences, and other arts-related disciplines. Always on the path to success!

In December 2023, with great excitement and pride, we had the honor of accompanying him to his graduation. Denny Michael graduated from the University of South Florida with a bachelor's degree in Media Communication, an achievement that filled our hearts with joy.

Denny Michael has been a true example of perseverance and courage. His life is filled with moments that remind us of the power of love, faith, and determination. From his childhood games to his academic achievements, Denny Michael has demonstrated exceptional courage to overcome challenges and move forward. Each chapter of his life is an inspiration to all who have the privilege of knowing him.

Denny Michael's infectious laughter, unwavering kindness, and passion for life are a gift from God that reminds us that even in the most challenging moments, there is light at the end of the tunnel. We are grateful for his brave spirit and the strength he inspires in all who surround him.

Now, as we reflect on all he has achieved, we cannot help but feel gratitude and admiration for the incredible man he has become. Denny Michael is more than a son, more than a brother, more than a friend; he is a true blessing.

And so, as we continue to celebrate his successes and share in his joy, we remember with gratitude the precious gift from God that is having Denny Michael in our lives. His story is a reminder that with faith, love, and determination, anything is possible.

Denny Michael, you are a true treasure, a beacon of hope, and a living example of what it means to be a miracle of life. We are infinitely grateful to God for the gift of having you in our lives and for the countless moments of joy and learning you have brought us. May your light continue to shine brightly, inspiring everyone around you to live each day with faith, passion, purpose, and gratitude.

www.ingramcontent.com/pod-product-compliance
Lightning Source LLC
Chambersburg PA
CBHW051605120626
46551CB00013B/1680